GOAL

Robert Burleigh

Illustrated by Stephen T. Johnson

Silver Whistle

Harcourt, Inc.

San Diego   New York   London

Printed in Hong Kong

Library of Congress Cataloging-in-Publication Data
Burleigh, Robert.
Goal/Robert Burleigh; illustrated by Stephen T. Johnson.
p. cm.
"Silver Whistle."
Summary: Illustrations and poetic text describe the movement and feel
of a fast-paced game of soccer.
1. Soccer—Juvenile poetry. 2. Children's poetry, American. [1. Soccer—
Poetry. 2. American poetry.] I. Johnson, Stephen, 1964– ill. II. Title.
PS3552.U7255G63 2001
811'.54—dc21 98-33181
ISBN 0-15-201789-5

The illustrations in this book were done in pastels on Lana Ingres paper.
The display type was set in Gothic.
The text type was set in Gagamond Bold.
Printed by South China Printing Company, Ltd., Hong Kong
This book was printed on totally chlorine-free Nymolla Matte Art paper.
Production supervision by Sandra Grebenar and Pascha Gerlinger

Score tied.
Muscles tense.
Ball drops.
After it—quick!

White spin-and-swirl.

Feet like fins

in dark green water.

Their ball! Get back!

River-wide field.

Flail of knees.

Splash of many legs.

Hold your position! Defense!

Players backpedaling.

Digging heels.

Explosions of gouged grass.

Mark tight! Guard the line!

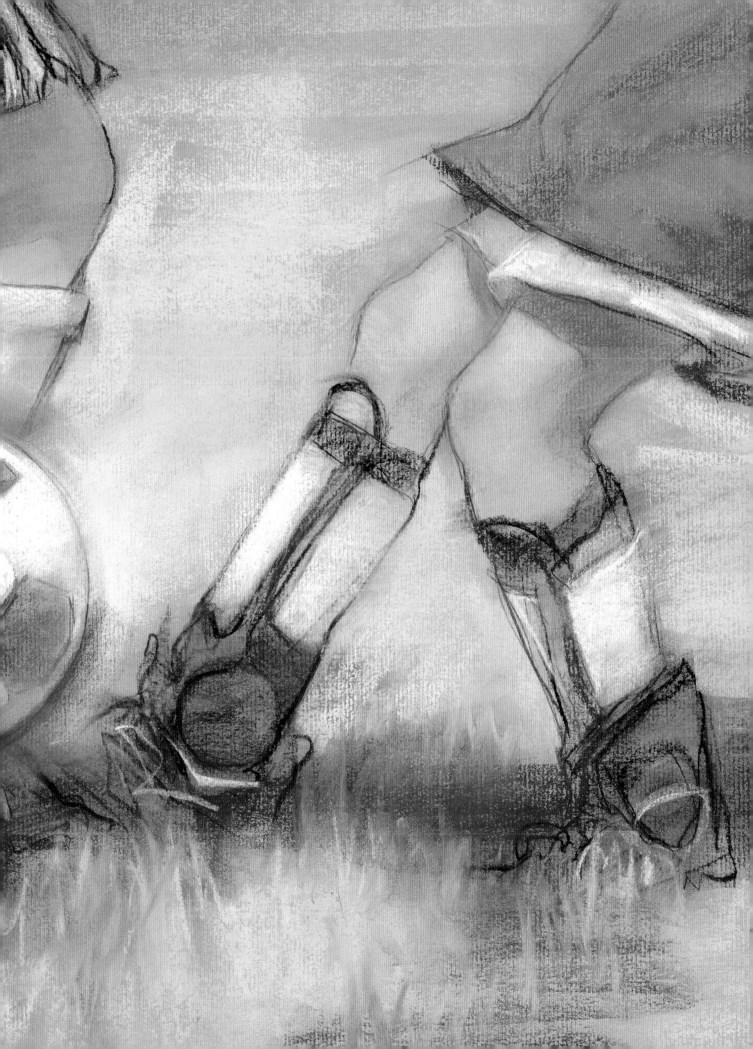

Crisscross. Flick.
And toe-tap quicker
than fingers opening.
My side! Mine!

Chip pass unspooling.

Boom off laces.

High as never-come-down.

Watch their scorer!

Corner kick curled and rising.

A pale rainbow.

Goaltender's catlike leap.

Great save! Clear it!

One minute left.
Last-second charge.
All wheeling as one.
Now! Make it happen!

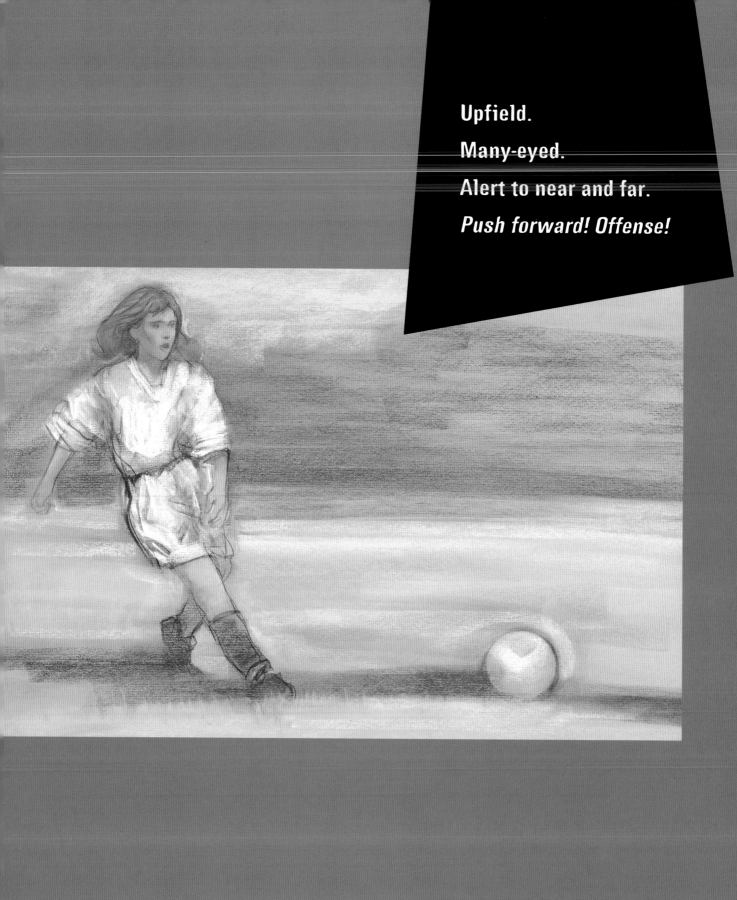

Upfield.

Many-eyed.

Alert to near and far.

Push forward! Offense!

Zig and zag.
Scrawl of leggy *Z*'s
on midfield air.
Here! Through!

Give and go.
Spinning inside.
Nearer and nearer.
I want—I want it!

Needle's-eye chink
in a wall of wild bodies.
The far post.
Launch it, striker!

Blur of whiteness.
Past goalie's single blink.
Suddenly, vibrating net.
See! See! Is it?

Leap for the sky.
Arms upraised.
Delirious dance.
We did it! We did it!

Goal.

Goal.

GOAL.

You, me, us—
champions.